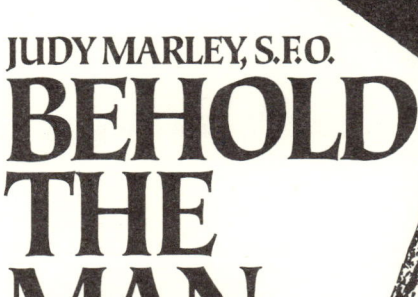

JUDY MARLEY, S.F.O.
BEHOLD THE MAN

Meditations on the Passion, Death and Resurrection of Jesus

Original edition published in 1990 by
Resurrection Press, Ltd.
P.O. Box 248
Williston Park, NY 11596
Revised edition published in 1997

Copyright © 1990 by Judy Marley, S.F.O.

ISBN 0-9623410-2-9

All rights reserved. No part of this book may be reproduced or transmitted in any form or by any means, electronic or mechanical, including photocopying, recording or by any information storage and retrieval system without permission in writing from the publisher.

Cover by John Murello

Inside illustrations by Jacqueline Seitz

Printed in the United States of America by Faith Printing

Contents

Introduction 1

Meditation One:
The Last Supper 5

Meditation Two:
The Garden 11

Meditation Three:
Betrayal and Denial 15

Meditation Four:
The Prisoner 21

Meditation Five:
Crowned and Beaten 27

Meditation Six:
Via Dolorosa 33

Meditation Seven:
Golgotha and Beyond 39

Introduction

Many of the Lord's faithful are devoted to meditating on the physical passion of Jesus during the Lenten season, and that is very good. However, I believe we should be aware of, and reflect often upon, the mental and emotional pain and sorrow which Jesus of Nazareth must have experienced during the ordeal he suffered during his last days on earth, not that we might feel pity for him, but so that we can have a deeper understanding and a greater appreciation of what our great God has done for each of us. In the climate of an active prayer life this will foster profound growth in our love and knowledge of the Lord Jesus, which in turn should bear the fruit of charity and understanding of one another, not only during Lent but every day of the year, year after year.

As we reflect on his emotional pain, we come to know that Jesus does not just understand our pain because he is God, but that he has *felt* our pain because he became human. His wounds are still open as he continues even now to feel our pain with us. Sometimes we assume that because Jesus Christ was God, the second Person of the Trinity, he was immune to disappointment, discouragement, fear and temptation. This is not so, and as we go on this truth will become clear.

The seven weeks of Lent can be seen as a season of great grace. During this time, following the rich tradition of our Church, most of the devotions we practice are based on Scripture and rounded out by Sacred Tradition and private revelation. This series of meditations is an attempt to read prayerfully between the lines to present a different look at the same mystery which has baffled people for over 1,900 years.

What we will do is to focus primarily on the emotional or mental passion which the Lord Jesus experienced, beginning with the time just before his Last Supper and ending at Golgotha when he was killed. As each of the seven events unfolds they will coincide with the seven weeks of Lent. Each individual meditation should be read, prayed and reflected on daily for one full week. The spirit of anticipation will build from week to week, until Holy Week, when the last meditation leads us to Golgotha and beyond, to the resurrection. The meditations, as read, place us outside of time and space as we become companions of Jesus during his walk of love.

These reflections are offered to you in the first person; that is, as Christ speaking personally to you as you accompany him through his mental passion. In no way are these meant to be prophetic, but simply the fruit of meditative prayer, entering into faith imagination. Jesus had an imagination, and he used it a great deal. As he has given each one of us an imagination too, we may feel free to use it sacramentally as a means of coming closer to him. So, seeing our endeavor as a journey into faith imagination, we should ask the Holy Spirit to bless and to walk with us in it.

Believe it or not there have been men and women who have suffered more than Jesus physically suffered. However, there has never been anyone born of a woman who has suffered more psychological stress or mental torture than Jesus. This is one aspect of his passion which we can all readily relate to. No matter what our culture, age, race or creed, we all suffer emotional stress and experience mental pain to some degree.

To have a fuller understanding of the meaning of the passion of Jesus, we first need to take a closer look at the mystery of the Incarnation. Crib and cross are inseparable, each part of the same glorious whole — Covenant Love. In the Gospel of St. John we read:

> In the beginning was the Word and the Word was in God's presence and the Word was God....The Word became flesh and made His dwelling among us. (Jn 1:1, 14)

The significant difference between just any man or woman suffering and Jesus suffering is the fact that he was God. Out of longing for union with his crown of creation he became a man and experienced the brokenness of humanity to facilitate the only means of reconciliation: the union in flesh of human and divine in the second Person of the One Triune God. The Incarnation is the very act of God himself becoming and being human, for humanity.

This man Jesus who fed the multitudes, himself went hungry. He who with a word controlled the elements was cold, wet and hot. He who walked on the water also walked miles and miles and became weary and exhausted. The man who spoke with profound eloquence and wisdom stood silent while unjustly accused. This same man who healed scores of people did not lift a finger to remove a single pain from his own mind or body. Jesus never used his powers for himself; he always used it to help others. This self-giving of our God is and should remain the example and the source of all acts of human love.

It was the Father's plan that the Lord experience humanity, and suffering is part of being human. Jesus saw this plan as perfect and chose to do his Father's will because it was his Father's will, no matter how horrendous it may have seemed. He chose to be broken and emptied, for so much did our God desire to identify with our weakness and our poverty, our bleeding, our pain and our tears, that he literally became one of us to be one with us: to be weak and poor, to bleed, to carry our pain, and to taste the salt in our tears.

This joining of the human and divine in Jesus Christ is what gives human nature its dignity, its only hope and the power to conquer evil in all its ugly forms. The uniting of his own pain to ours gives our pain a new, eternal dimension. All the sorrow, pain, frustration and grief we experience as we sojourn here on earth are infinitely meaningless unless joined to his one great and constant act of self-giving. When we unite ourselves to his mysterious passion our own emotional pain is divinized, for God himself sanctified it.

Scripture tells us that for some time before his last trip to Jerusalem, Jesus knew that trouble was imminent. He was fully human in all things but sin, so naturally the thoughts and anticipation of what his life was moving towards and the painful reflections regarding that must have been torturous at times. It is specifically his human nature — his thoughts, fears, disappointments, frustrations, temptations — and how we can relate them to our own struggle to live the life we are called to live, that we will be contemplating during this time of intense reflection.

A SUGGESTION:

If these meditations are read aloud — in a prayer group, for example — the effect will be enhanced if two different speakers participate, one for the voice of Jesus and one for the narration.

MEDITATION ONE

The Last Supper

OUR FIRST meditation takes place at the Last Supper. The scene is a familiar one. As we enter the spacious upper room we can see two long tables forming an "L" as they are placed together. Some of the apostles have not arrived yet, but most of them are present. Those who are there seem to be engaged in heated conversations, deciding about the preparations and comparing this room and its accommodations to the place where they celebrated last year's Passover. Others are rushing around getting things ready for the meal. Some are fearfully discussing their association with Jesus as they speculate about a possible arrest; still others are debating over which one of them is most important. There is one man in the room who is not joining in these conversations. He is reclining alone at the center of the larger table. He is Jesus. With affectionate and tender eyes he intently looks at the other men in the room. He seems in a way to be sad, although the atmosphere in the room around him is anything but somber. We approach him, unseen by the others, and he looks up and speaks to us.

Shalom aleikhem, peace be with you, my friend; welcome. I have brought you here because you have desired to be a comfort to me in my passing. It is my desire to share a portion of this bittersweet meal with you, to help you understand the things which are to come.

This Passover night is quite different from any other Passover night. All at once, this is the Last Passover of the Old Covenant and the First Meal of the New Covenant. This is the beginning of my own passing from life to death to life. As this is a night I choose to share with my most intimate friends, it is fitting that you are here.

As I lie here at table waiting for it all to begin, looking at my friends, seeing their actions, I know I must pray all the more that they will soon grasp the reality which I have daily tried to teach them. This is a momentous night indeed, and everything that will happen here has deep meaning and purpose. The promise of eternal deliverance is being fulfilled before their very eyes! This meal is not just a remembrance of one saving act over and long past, but the celebration of an ongoing deliverance, alive, given and sustained by my Father for the past, present and future.

My frustration is greatly increased by the knowledge that the significance of tonight will escape my friends. They have been fearful, frustrated and confused so often because I have not been afraid to speak the truth out in the open, and because what I teach them is so far above human logic and reason. I don't mind telling you I have been frustrated more than once by their lack of understanding. My comfort now is in knowing that in time, they will understand.

You are proof of that.

The bond of friendship I have formed with each of these men is symbolic of the relationships I will be able to have with many others very soon. How I long for that time! Look at them, I love them so. I know each and every one intimately — their strengths and their faults.

I know how frightened they are when I speak out publicly against hypocrisy and declare, for all to hear, who I am.

I know that they get on one another's nerves from time to time and how they bicker among themselves.

However, only a short time from now, through my own life flowing in them, they will learn how unimportant their fears, ambitions, and disagreements are. My friends are so dear to me; I have such a deep affection for each of them. I not only love each one, but I like them. I enjoy their company; being with them brings me great pleasure. Just as a mother loves her children do I love each of them. It is difficult for me to realize that I must leave them soon. We have spent so much time together; it is as if we are already one body.

But later I will return to them, although they don't believe that or even understand now, because their faith is so feeble. Soon they will go through a necessary time of purging and testing and I won't be there, physically, to help them through it. Their faith in me will be shaken and sorely tried

— all but one will come out stronger.

I have done my best with them, and I have also tried not to show them my own fear and apprehension, because they are so very weak, so very fragile. Their hearts would simply burst with pain and grief if they knew what I know. They haven't really seen what I have seen, nor have they yet been given what I have been given. Even though I know this, from time to time I am tempted to expect more from them than they are able to give.

In the midst of celebration there is great sadness in knowing the secrets of another's heart. At times I would rather not know all that I know, for the weight of hypocrisy and deception are heavy upon my heart now.

Over there is the one who will betray me. His name is Judas. He is standing alone because the others don't like him very much, but I do. I love him. As a matter of fact, if he could only comprehend just how much I do love him, he could be saved from his destiny.

This is a night I have greatly looked forward to with pleasure and which, at the same time, I have anticipated with fear. As I look into the faces of my friends, I am keenly aware that in this one meal I have so very much to accomplish. By word, action, attitude and example I must leave them with a lasting impression of the meaning of my life here and its significance to them — indeed, its significance to all of creation! Tonight by deed, I write my own eulogy.

In my heart of hearts I long to wash and stroke their feet in gratitude as I remember all the dusty roads we traveled together, the hours of laughter and joy we have all shared, the worry, the disappointments we have known, the excitement over the miracles and the bold attacks on sin. We have been tired and weary together for my Father's purpose and it has been good. I am glad to have spent that time with them. It is the desire of my heart to be truly one with them, as my Father and I are one.

Once again, my friends will be shocked when I ask them to drink my blood and eat my body. However, I must let them know that I freely give up my life for them — for all — and in this way I will be a real part of them as they eat and drink and become a part of me. As they consume my body and blood they share not only in my life, but in my suffering, as I share in theirs. For it is only through my life — blood and spirit — that they will be cleansed from the inside out and share in eternal life.

I can think of no better way to demonstrate to them that I have come to serve than by donning the apron and washing their feet, as the lowest of the house servants would do. There is no better way to indicate how I must cleanse them. By this, in time, they will see how they must then wash and cover one another in humility.

Likewise, I can think of no better way to leave behind a testimony of my final and all-encompassing sacrifice, than to reserve a portion of my own body and blood to be shared by all my people as long as time exists.

My thoughts are with Judas once again. I remember the first day I looked into his eyes; he came to me so full of excitement and zeal. But his zeal wasn't for Father's kingdom, but for a material kingdom which would impress and eventually oppress people. I tried to show him that I sought to free people, not to oppress them; to serve, not to impress.

I am grieved and greatly saddened to look at him now. He is no different from anyone else here, in that they have all misunderstood my coming and my message. Tonight he will sit by my side; I will wash his feet and share my body and blood with him. Forgiveness is already his if he would but receive it, but he will not, so my heart aches for him.

Looking at them all now, I know what lies ahead, not only for me, but for each one of them also. Thus has my passion already begun, even before tonight. Just knowing beforehand what I must do — anticipating it all, knowing what my mother will suffer, and knowing what my friends will go through — is all part of the cross I already carry. Just as my Father strengthened me on the Mount of Transfiguration before I came here, so too do I pray he will strengthen them as well.

Yet the same three who witnessed my glory on the Mount are still oblivious to what is about to take place. Those same three will leave me comfortless later tonight. But then, no human understands all that I am going through. In reality, only my Father knows the secrets of my heart and the thoughts of my mind. He alone knows the full extent of my pain and suffering at this moment.

Are you surprised by the conflict you see in me? Do the

fears, pain, frustration and temptations you witness in me shock you? You needn't be shocked, friend, for my vulnerability is my greatest strength. I want you to know that my emotional pain is deep, for I came down to be fully human and I bear these kinds of pains with you...for you.

It is time now for you to depart. We will meet later in the olive garden, but for now everyone is here and we are ready to begin the meal. Until later. *Shalom.*

MEDITATION TWO
The Garden

OUR SECOND *meditation takes place in the garden of Gethsemane. In faith imagination we recall that Jesus asked us to meet him here, so we enter the garden. Immediately we sense an eerie silence shrouding the place. Although there is a gentle breeze blowing through the trees, we notice a profound stillness there. As we look around we can see why Jesus often chose this place for prayer, particularly tonight. It is a lovely orchard, a place which quietly speaks of the beauty and glory of the Creator. The ancient olive trees and their lovely scent hold a promise of order and timeless serenity in the midst of the conflict and confusion of this night.*

As we walk along we pass a group of men asleep and we recognize some of them as the disciples of Jesus, but he is not among them. As we continue on our search for him, we come upon a small clearing and on the side we see three men half asleep; we know them as Peter, James and John. We pass them by, for they are not the reason why we were brought here.

Then we hear a noise coming through the trees — it seems to be someone groaning or crying. About twenty feet away, in the moonlight, we see a figure bent over what seems to be a large rock. It is Jesus. We hesitate to go any farther, for he is obviously in great distress. He turns our way and invites us to come closer.

Shalom aleikhem, peace, my friend. See, I am all alone; don't be afraid to draw near to me in my distress, it will bring me comfort if you come. Here, sit by me. I've brought you here tonight because I have many things to share with you.

You saw my friends as you came in; they have been through so much already. I hunger for their companionship at this time, but their bodies are very tired; emotionally they are drained and full of fear. I've asked them here tonight so that they could pray with me, but they cannot. My need for their comfort now does not outweigh their need, so I will continue to pray my Father's strength into them for what lies ahead.

I, too, am very tired; in fact I am exhausted, and my mind gives me no rest at all. With or without my friends I will have no lasting rest or comfort until it is finished. Fear oppresses me as my mind becomes immersed in a whirlpool of suffering.

I see now before my eyes a panorama of horror. It is the awful reality of sin — past, present and future. I am utterly repulsed by the perversion I see; it fills my mind, and for the first time I feel as if I am separated from my Father as this vision of evil crashes in upon me. I feel that I am being wrenched from his breast.

What unspeakable pain! How can I look at so much evil and still see my Father and his beauty? I cannot see or feel his love, so I feel myself shrinking back from that which I must do. I have always experienced his strength and support, even in the midst of my trials in the desert. He is with me, though it would seem as if he is gone. I feel torn from him as I am united and joined more fully to suffering humanity.

This sword cuts deeply into my heart and begins to drain the resolve from me. So, I ask, "Father, let this cup pass me by." Never has he denied his favor to me, for my will has always been at one with his. My plea comes from the very depths of my tortured human soul.

Feeling as I do, utterly alone in the midst of all this evil, I am acutely aware of the responsibility which has been given to me. It is what I am, it is what I came for; this pain which I take upon myself, which I carry deep within my heart, is your pain, and that of all humanity. Looming in my thoughts are the atrocities that the Son of Man must endure for this, not as a sacrifice to appease an angry god, but as a ransom for a loving and tender Father.

I can tell you, because you are my true friend. I am frightened. I don't look forward to my flesh being ripped and torn open. Although much physical pain lies ahead, it cannot compare to the agony I suffer now. I don't want to go through that kind of suffering; there must be other ways to achieve the goal....

The anguish now is almost more than I can bear; I have

the chance to flee this place, to run from this, to refuse the cup.... But no, something profoundly present in my depths — my love for my Father, my love for you — the two are inseparable — this love will endure and overcome the temptations and conflict in my mind.

My friend, you are here, with me. You are my only comfort at this moment. Thank you for coming. In this agony you are an angel of mercy sent by my Father. It is your love, your faithfulness and your loyalty to me that give me comfort in this torture. So all the more, now that you are in my sight, I must pray and travail, for in you I see what could be possible for all, and I see that the price is not too high.

I am like a woman in labor; my head could burst from the pressure, it throbs so. In my heart I place all humanity's pain, all the fear, all the loneliness, the rejection, every sorrow, every injustice. Every single victim of sin has filled my heart; it breaks wide open with their pain so that every pore in my body gives birth to drops of blood. I shed it for them. I shed it for you.

It is not the heavy hand of another which forces this death upon me; it is my own choice. It is the heavy burden of sin upon me as I feel the pain of the suffering multitudes which squeezes the life-blood from my body.

My angel, my friend, wipe this blood from my face so I may see you clearly once more before you go. As I lean upon this rock, shining through your love for me I see my Father. He is my strength, my only strength. In the midst of all this I cling to the truth which is obscured by this darkness — that he is with me, and that in my aloneness and abandonment I am neither abandoned nor alone. I take and accept the cup of his holy will; I drink deeply and its taste is not bitter at all, it is so very sweet. I embrace what lies ahead, for I walk not the way of sorrow, but the way of love.

Thank you, my friend, for this moment of relief you have brought to me. You are at once my gift to my Father and now his gift to me. You are aglow with his love for me.

Now you must leave me for a time, as I must be alone again to labor for all those who cannot hear my cry of pain or my shout of victory. I must pray now for my friends again; for Judas, for Peter, for you...for myself.

Please meet me at the edge of the garden in another hour. Until then, my angel. *Shalom.*

Meditation Three
Betrayal and Denial

OUR THIRD meditation takes place near the edge of the Garden of Gethsemane. Jesus has arranged to meet us there, so we enter the garden a little way and wait for him to come. The hour is late and the garden itself is very quiet. The night sky is exceptionally clear and full of stars. We hear the sound of slow but steady footsteps coming in our direction, and in the bluish glow of the moonlit night we see Jesus as he approaches. He looks gravely troubled, although we would have expected him to look much worse, knowing, as we do, what he had just gone through. There is something different about his manner now: his prayer has renewed him somehow. There is an air of control and great strength emanating from him, even in the midst of his apparent brokenness. He holds his arms open wide and tenderly greets us with a kiss and a strong, drawn-out embrace.

Shalom aleikhem, my beloved. I knew you would come. I want you to know how sincerely I appreciate your readiness to be available to me, to be a comfort to this body, to be a friend to the Son of Man. Our bond is so intimate, that as I first shared in your plight and your sufferings, so do you share in mine. You are here because you are a part of my broken body, and through my passion you can glimpse your own humanity and see that when joined with my divinity, even you can overcome any spiritual, emotional or physical difficulty or distress.

We haven't much time; soon I will have to wake the others from their sleep because my hour has come. Although my garden agony has passed, my prayers are by no means finished, for now I enter into a different form of prayer. All I do from this point on will be prayer — for me, for you and for all. Indeed my actions are the greatest and most perfect of all prayers.

The soldiers approach quickly, as does my betrayer. In only a few moments' time this quiet moonlit respite will be ablaze — not with the flames of their torches, but with the fires of violence, ambition, fear and pride. It is hard to imagine that this stillness, so reminiscent of the peace which has always been in my heart, will be violated and shattered by the noise and clamor of weapons, shields and the footgear of war.

The moment of truth moves swiftly towards us. My heart still throbs when I realize that almost all of my friends will desert me, one of my closest friends will outright deny me and the one whom I trusted with the common fund has already sold me for the price of a month's wages, the cost of a slave at market.

Tonight, a kiss and a hug become the symbol of betrayal. Can you not see how sin perverts and distorts the pure and the true? Can you not see now why I come to this hour readily, in spite of my fear? It is my destiny to bear witness to the true and the pure, and so empower others to walk the way of love and truth bravely.

Betrayal is a most difficult experience to endure. Rejection of any sort is deeply grievous, but is particularly so when inflicted by one whom you love. An act of betrayal is not hard to perform when one is full of pride and self-will like Judas. For such a one, self-justification comes very easily.

Although I am tempted to lash out at Judas, I will choose to embrace him, for I have always shown him love and truth and I can do nothing less — even now. He will not remember my words. This is a burden of heavy proportion. At the thought of it my heart pounds as I feel the heat of deep hurt and anger well up across my head and chest.

He will come, leading the soldiers to me.

He will embrace me with arms of deceit.

He will look directly into my eyes and call me "friend."

Even now my eyes fill and overflow with tears as I think of what his look will reveal. For in his eyes I will see death — not only mine, but his as well. My death will lead to freedom over sin and bring reconciliation with my Father to you, to my friends here, and to those yet to come. But the death pall in his eyes reveals his own damnation. For his self-will in due time will give birth to self-pity, and his pride will give way to despair.

If only he could see past himself for a moment and believe all I have taught him, all I have shown him, he would know that he, too, is hidden in the open wound of love within my heart, for Judas is not my enemy; that which possesses and drives him to betray me, that is my enemy. Sin. I have come to conquer sin, not Judas.

At this time I am deeply troubled by the thought of the desertion which will soon take place. The fear which will take hold and grip my friends is now greater and stronger than their faithfulness and trust in me. I must plead with the guards for their safety and release, for now they are simply unable to cope. They are so much like children and I find that my overriding desire now is to protect them any way I can.

After the Comforter comes to them, their faithfulness and courage will be master over their instinctive fear and weakness. But for now, they will abandon me and leave me utterly alone in all of this. I must be alone, though, for my patient enduring of this intense abandonment will win for them, and for all who come, a place in my Father's family, so that they will never be alone or abandoned or rejected.

My thoughts now turn to Peter, my rock. Tonight he will be more like a little pebble. His moment of truth will not be when he denies his master, but afterwards, as he sees what sin allows him to be capable of, no matter what his intent. His spirit is willing but his flesh is weak. However, he will remember my words and live them. He will repent of his denial. His own self-will will break and become true sorrow and contrition. His pride will melt away in my love and forgiveness.

Knowing how it will all turn out still does not mitigate the pain as I anticipate how my friends will leave me. It hurts me very deeply. Human nature is very weak, and even as the human will was crucified here in this garden, so too will the fallen human nature be put to death at the cross — only to rise again from the tomb of death, transformed in me and with me.

Listen, hear the noise of the soldiers coming now. My friends are not even awake yet, so I must go. As the sounds get louder, my already bruised and battered heart races and momentarily I am filled with dread. For men who do not know me at all will lay their hands upon me and bind me;

they will lead me to be questioned, ridiculed, abused, and misunderstood — and finally, to be tortured further and condemned to a cruel and painful death.

Although I could command a legion of angels to come to my rescue, I will not use violence to accomplish my purpose. I will be as meek as a lamb as they arrest me and allow them to lead me to the slaughter. I choose this, for it is my Father's way and as such it is my way.

It is time for you to leave me also, for I must go to embrace Judas, and accept the embrace of greed, deceit and pride. For in the arms of his sin I will be accepting and embracing the pain and suffering of all humanity in one more way. In him I embrace all those who will betray anyone, all those motivated by pride or ambition. As I embrace him I let him and them know that forgiveness is possible in my embrace.

I know it is your desire to stay with me, to comfort me, to spare me, but it cannot be like that. Nothing you can do can stop this. Indeed, no one should attempt to stop these tragic yet glorious events from unfolding. For if they did, I would use all my power to stop their misdirected attempts to change the outcome of this night. As a matter of fact, it is for this very reason that I will use my power only once more before my death to heal the ear of another servant.

Go now my child, my beloved. I am ready. Later tonight I will call you to come to me after my appearance before the High Priest. Until then, *shalom.*

Meditation Four

The Prisoner

THE NEXT step on our journey into faith imagination takes place after the trial of Jesus before the high priest Caiaphas, the Sanhedrin, and Caiaphas' father-in-law Annas, but before his trial by Pontius Pilate, the Roman Prefect of Judea. We find ourselves in a very dark room. It is cold and damp. We cannot stand upright because the ceiling in the room is too low. As we are bent over, all at once we are nauseated by a horrible stench which fills the air in the place. It is dreary and quite depressing.

As our eyes become accustomed to the darkness surrounding us, we see the figure of a man sitting on the mud floor, leaning up against the wall. At first he is barely visible in the darkness, but as we cautiously move a little closer we are stunned to realize it is Jesus our Master. His hands and feet are tied and bound with ropes. As we begin to grasp this unspeakable sight we rush over to him and kneel by his side, overwhelmed by the urge to untie the ropes. He looks into our eyes and we are halted by his penetrating gaze. In his soft, dark eyes we see love, sadness, tenderness, pain, power, mercy, understanding and peace, all in just one glance into his eyes, as they reflect the beauty and the truth of his very soul to us. We are locked into his gaze and we are lost, for a moment and for what seems like all of time itself. He then speaks to us.

    Peace be upon you, my beloved friend. The night is almost spent and the dawn very soon will be upon us. The evil of the long dark night will soon be enveloped by the power of my light. Here in this, my prison of rejection, I would share some thoughts with you to help on your journey as you share in mine.

    Some journeys get easier as they approach their goal; that is not so with this one. This journey which I am allowing you to share will become more difficult as we move ahead. That is why so few choose to follow this way.

Yet it is not for the purpose of focusing on my own pain that I share these memories with you — not just to stir up your pity, although greater compassion will be one benefit of this walk with me. I already know that I am the object of your love. I want you to know that the purpose for this and every other journey I lead you on is to bring you an ever deepening love and understanding of my own love for you. If you learn the lessons I try to teach you, you will be blessed.

This has been a very long and trying night for me. I am weary and utterly exhausted, but I cannot rest at all. The trial before the high priest and the elders was extremely difficult to endure. Even before I arrived I was emotionally drained and experiencing deep sadness. So intense is my mental pain that it has affected me physically, although as I stood before them they saw me as a man fully composed.

Even in the midst of their insults and bodily abuses, even when they spat right into my face, although repulsed by this, I remained calm. For since the garden I have become my prayer. For me everything I do is prayer and it was only my Father and his generous strength which allowed me to stand before my own people as they lied about me and falsely accused me.

Ironically their own high priest questioned me, the eternal High Priest. Yet all must learn that it is not the blood of an animal or the title of a person or anything else which will bring their everlasting forgiveness and deliverance, but only the love and life-blood of their God, sacrificed in me, made holy and offered by me. It is only this which will make all other sacrifices holy and acceptable.

As I stood before the Sanhedrin ready to collapse, I was tempted to cry out, to quote every scripture, to show them an undeniable sign. But now, the Son of Man had to embrace this further betrayal. You see, my beloved, these men were all learned in the Holy Writings and Scriptures; they saw me, they knew my message and they have seen my works, and I am just as their prophets foretold.

They knew, but they wouldn't accept. Although there were some present there, even men of position and rank, who believed in me, they were afraid to speak out forcibly for fear of their own positions. This is why Pilate will bend to the demands of the high priest and Sanhedrin and condemn me.

This mock trial and unjust judgment — much more than the appearance I will soon make before Pilate, and even more than the humiliations I will suffer at the hands of Herod — is most painful, simply because these are my chosen people, children of Abraham, children of faith. Where is their faith? In the past, as a nation they rejected all attempts which my Father made to speak his words to them. Now he sends his Word once again, not just through any man, but his own Word become flesh in THE man. They still reject, and this causes untold grief in my heart; and so I continually ask my Father to forgive them, for they really do not know or understand what they are doing.

Still, I love them as I love myself, and it is only all of this which will make it possible for them to come to full and complete restoration. Israel — indeed, all humanity and the whole of creation — will be reconciled and glorified in me, because I am broken and emptied out, and with dignity and grace I accept this, my prison of rejection, and embrace it with arms of divine and sacred love.

As I told you earlier, my beloved, this is another lesson for you to learn: that now, as my Father's child, you too can do the same when you are ridiculed or treated unfairly. When you choose to embrace your malefactors with the arms of my love I will pour my own grace and strength and dignity into you; and your inability will become my ability, your weakness will become my strength and you will be free to love and embrace even your enemies and those who betray you.

As I sit here and anticipate what still lies ahead, I am filled with apprehension and pity. I can almost hear the clamor of the words ringing in my ears. Soon the crowds will shout to have me crucified when Pilate displays me in such a sorry state.

I wonder at it all. Where are the thousands I fed, where are those whom I've healed and delivered, all those whom I taught about the kingdom of love?

This city is now filled with pilgrims from all over the country as they come to celebrate the feast of deliverance, the Passover. It is also filled with many whom I've touched in one way or another, many who will never be the same again because of my touch. However, their voices will not be heard over the loud, full-throated cry of evil, "Crucify him!" These slaves to passion are pitiable, for sin is their only master, and it is for them that I willingly lie here bound and tightly tied like a criminal.

I see that these ropes bother you, but I will not allow you to loosen them for me, for they are symbols, and in them I see all the evil that has bound you and all humanity for so long. Without reluctance I am bound a prisoner here, for I share in and I intimately know the bondage of humanity.

Soon I will release humanity's ropes and chains of fear and sorrow. I have come to knock down the prisons which have no walls except in the hearts and minds of my suffering people. Know this well and as I tell you now, go and tell them that it is in the depth of my broken, sorrowful heart that they will find my unfailing consolation. It is in the depth of my own painful passion where they will find their source of strength and freedom.

These men here do not even know what they are about, let alone what I am about, so how can they know what it is they do? Even those who will mock me and blindfold me and make sport of me do not really know what they are doing. People will continue to mock me until I come again, but this too is a hardship to bear, another humiliation I peaceably accept in order to bring God's love fully to this earth. I do walk this way of love joyfully, if you can try to understand that. It will enable the pure light of truth finally to shine forth out of the darkness in human hearts and minds.

It is traumatic for me to experience this pain of rejection and ridicule. Yet my fulfillment and peace do not depend on such things as human esteem — for I know who I am; I know where I come from and where I am going. What they say about me cannot change the truth.

But my love and longing for these people is so great that their taunting and mocking pierce me like poison arrows, ripping and tearing my soul from within, even more violently than they will tear the flesh of my body with their despicable weapons.

The time is nearly upon us when the guards will take me before Pilate — to be judged by a Gentile. Now even as both Jew and Gentile will have a share in my death, so too will both Jew and Gentile be able to share in my triumph. Soon I will see my friend, Peter, one last painful time before my death. He will see much in my eyes, just as you did, only he will see the reflection of his own failure as he looks helplessly at me in my apparent failure.

Very soon now I will be mocked and brutally whipped almost to the point of death, until they grow bored of the cruel inhuman game.

You must leave me now and trust our dear Father with me in this and in everything. I will bring you back to me later. Meanwhile, ponder all I have shared with you here and pray that you will be open and receptive to what I want to teach you. Until then, my beloved, *shalom*.

MEDITATION FIVE
Crowned and Beaten

OUR NEXT meditation takes place in the courtyard of the Praetorium of Pontius Pilate. A new day has dawned and it is early morning. There is much activity going on. Guards are marching; horses being fed, exercised and groomed; weapons being checked and prisoners being moved about. There is a lot of noise around this palace because the city is bustling with pilgrims for the feast. Crowds are gathering around the fortress expecting to see another bloody spectacle. The word has already gotten out that there is to be another public execution today. We find ourselves standing in the center of the large open yard. In the midst of all this movement we notice a crowd of rowdy soldiers gathered in one spot over by the side wall of one of the large buildings. They are laughing and obviously having a lot of fun, slapping each other on the back all the while as they are joking.

Unseen, we move a little closer to see what is going on. One by one they move out of the way as they seem to tire of the sport and we see the object of their laughter. They are laughing at a man. The poor creature looks wretched. As we look at him more closely, we realize that this man is our Lord, Jesus.

As he leans there against the wall, half slumped over and practically falling, we notice that he is covered from head to foot by gashes and wounds from the beating he has just received. We barely recognize him. He hardly resembles the strong and comely man we remember meeting in the upper room.

The soldiers, as we can now deduce, were mocking his kingship. They have covered his bloody and bruised body with a torn red rag and have put a large branch of sorts in his arms, as a mock royal robe and scepter. They have also "crowned" him with a sort of cap made from a very sharp and thorny shrub. We can see that this has cut *deeply into his scalp, because his hair is now matted together as the blood soaks it and continually runs, dripping down over his bruised and swollen face and neck.*

We wonder why he would let us see him this way. We wonder how these people could do this to another human being.

Although he does not look as he did before, his eyes are still a penetrating world within themselves. His glance cuts us like a sword. As he looks up, his eyes tell us that he intimately knows the conflict in our minds at this point. His breathing very labored, he speaks to us.

Shalom aleikhem, my beloved. Do not let my appearance frighten you. Come over here, closer to me. I understand your conflict, your discouragement, your fear and apprehension. I am feeling these emotional knives as well. Look at your God. See how he humbles himself once again. I have come to be bound, beaten down and made helpless, for that is the awful reality of what sin does to human beings and only in me can people attain freedom from that condition.

My friend, it is important that you sufficiently understand the fact of my humanity. In me, God and man have wed. In me, one may behold brokenness and wholeness at the same time. Into your brokenness I bring my wholeness, and in my own brokenness you are made whole. My Father made you in his image, and he in turn made himself in your image out of love, to empathize, to identify compassionately with your pain, to take on the full weight of it in order to give you a way out of it. The Son of God became human so that humans could become the children of God.

I suffer thus to give you a most precious treasure, a gift beyond price — the Paraclete. I know that without this gift it is impossible for anyone to imitate me and live my humble way of love or to overcome sin. My enslavement is the price of human freedom. My patient endurance means that you need never be bound by your sinfulness. Through my suffering comes the gift which is the very source of and also the fruit of my labor, the personification and indwelling presence of the love Father and I have shared since before the world even began — our Holy Spirit.

I know that you have read and prayed much about my

physical torment so I will not dwell on that. Although I know my physical pain will greatly increase, extreme mental torture and ungodly temptations still persist, even in the midst of this ocean of physical suffering. That in itself increases my emotional turmoil even more.

As I lie here up against this wall waiting, I see before me a trail of bloodstained footprints. I am tempted to be discouraged, for as I look ahead, I look behind as well — and I am painfully aware that what I have actually accomplished thus far was not enough. Not everyone was drawn closer to my Father, not everyone was made whole, not everyone responded to me. Even after the great gift is poured out, even then not everyone will come.

I have done my absolute best, I have glorified my Father by my life, I have loved completely. Even though my heart is so caught up in the results of my ministry and the fruit of my work here, I must detach myself even from that and look only to my Father now, for his love compels me to continue with this. My thirst and love for him and my love and longing for all people will endure, for our love never fails.

I thought it next to impossible that the pain already present in my head could increase — that is, until they thrust this thorny crown upon me. I willingly accept it, for just as thorns and thistles were part of Adam's punishment, I take his punishment upon myself as graciously as a king receives his crown. I receive this painful crown as a symbol of all the mental anguish which sin has allowed into the world. For just as these men have taken and twisted this plant, which is one of my Father's creations, and used it for an evil purpose, so too, has Satan taken the human race, the crown of my Father's creation, and perverted it through sin.

I will lay down my life, I will do anything to remove this burden from humanity. Although I know all of this in my heart and mind, my human nature rises up and the pain, the sorrow and the sickening reality of evil overwhelm me. I wrench as my emotions well up within, while the tempter comes once again to torment me in my weakened condition.

In the midst of all these people, I am rejected and feel absolutely alone. The closer I get to my altar, the more separate I feel from my Father. As I think about what lies ahead, will this body make it? Yes, my Father would not have brought me to this point only to abandon me. No matter how I feel, I know he is with me; we are one. The weakness of this flesh I carry would be too much to bear if it were not for his life in me. As he fills me with strength in the midst of this grave distress, because of my total openness to him you will be enabled to be filled by his grace and power in your own trials.

Amid all this activity I have a deep sense of abandonment. As the blood drips down my forehead, it dries and crusts around my eyes; it is difficult to see clearly. I look for a familiar face, but I do not recognize anyone here. I don't see my friends, or my mother, or anyone whom I've healed — none are familiar to me here. There are soldiers but they bring no relief; they taunt, laugh, mock and jeer. Even in the midst of all the noise and all the people here, I am so alone.

Once again the thought of you and your love for me is of great comfort now. But do not allow yourself to take pride in this. Do not be too quick to judge these men for what they do. For you, indeed all people are capable of inflicting great pain upon one another unless you are open to my grace.

This is another reason why I continually pray and ask my Father to forgive them, to forgive you. Their obscene behavior is just a further misuse and perversion of the gift of free will. The great gift of my Father to humanity is now used as a weapon against me. At the trial they accused me of being a friend to sinners and they were correct; I am. You know that to be so, for I am your greatest friend, even as I am theirs. The only difference is that you know it, and only by the grace of my Father.

My friend, I know your love for me is genuine and that you do not desire to see me suffer so. I accept this tender comfort from you, and at the same time remind you that what you do to the least of my brothers and sisters you do to me. There is only so much that can be accomplished in three years' time, and although I will soon win the war, there are many skirmishes still to be fought.

By the treasure within, you and I are one. Offer your hardship and pain in me as I offer mine in you, and I will sanctify them. Do not hurt me by misusing your gift of free will at the expense of another. Gracefully forgive the faults and sins of others as I have so gracefully forgiven yours.

As you see me suffering and laboring to be born more fully in your brothers and sisters, minister to me hidden within them as you minister to me now, when my glory is hidden behind my brokenness. Do not be like the man who contemptuously thrust these thorns of anguish upon my head, but be like the one who will gently remove them from my body out of love. Both were cut by the same instrument of pain, but each for a different motive and purpose.

As I reflect on what is to come my heart pounds so loudly that I can hear the pulsation in my ears. In just a moment they will come and I will begin my gloriously agonizing walk. I will not send you away this time, for as I carry my cross, I invite you to go with me along the via dolorosa. Look at me once more and do not cringe or shrink back from what I ask. As you gaze upon me now you can easily see how I can say,

"Come to me: I am no stranger to pain, disgrace, discouragement, fear and frustration. I am a man well acquainted with sorrow, yet my pain has not made me bitter, so I am gentle and compassionate of heart. You who are burdened will find rest and comfort in my weary arms. I first shared your pain, and because you live in me you share in mine. Take my yoke; it is not too hard, for I carry the load with you."

As you walk the way of the cross with me, I will show you how to carry your own crossbeam. You will see that the burden I gently lay upon your shoulders is light because mine is so very heavy.

Meditation Six
Via Dolorosa

BELOVED, do you remember when I told you that this journey would get more difficult as we progressed? Now you will graphically see the price paid for your salvation and the true cost of discipleship. I have allowed you to be here because you will learn much of value upon this rough and stony road with me. You will see how to be my follower.

Just as I will not leap and skip down this road to Golgotha, neither do you on your own way of the cross. You will fall even as I will fall here, but take courage; for I promise you I will never leave you for even an instant, and I will carry the load with you.

I have something very special for you to do now. I want you to think of that sin or person or situation which most burdens you at this time, whether it be sin, sorrow, sickness, frustration or weakness. Symbolically, place it into your hands and put it down on the ground over there.

Jesus points to a pile of wood. We do as he tells us, and as we stand there we see that our burden is transformed in the blink of an eye into a very large beam of wood. We are shocked and filled with disbelief, so we bend over to touch it to see if it is real. We then attempt to pick it up, but we cannot, because it is much too heavy. Jesus says,

Do not be surprised, for it is within my power to turn the abstract into the very real. All things are possible in me. Perhaps this small gesture will enable you to understand more fully what I will do for you here as I walk the path laid out before me.

Immediately, quite a few soldiers come over to him and one of them grabs him roughly by the hair and pulls him to his feet. Another rips off the torn military cloak from his back and he winces from the pain, because it has dried into his many wounds and now painfully reopens them. Someone unties his hands and tells him to hurry and get dressed in his own clothes right there. Unable to wait, he gruffly helps Jesus along. Anxious to receive the day's wage, the soldier impatiently hits Jesus on the top of the head and shoulder with the flat edge of his sword, driving the thorns even deeper and causing another gash in his flesh. When he is half dressed they throw a sign around his neck which reads, "Jesus of Nazareth, King of the Jews."

Two soldiers then go to the pile of wood and pick up a large beam. It is the one which we placed there; it is our burden. The men struggle as they carry it and forcibly thrust it upon his shoulders. Jesus' legs buckle under its weight, but he regains his stance and holds it upon his shoulders. Then they wrap a rope around the wood and his body, and with other prisoners and many soldiers he is led out of the courtyard, out into the mobbed streets where he is assailed by unbridled ridicule and laughter.

As the unruly crowds make way for the "procession" we walk — unseen — by his side. The road itself is very rough and uneven. His clothes are now soaked with blood as it drips its indictment upon the streets of Jerusalem, just as the burden on his back indicts us.

Because he is so weak and wounded he loses his balance, and as they push him along he falls. The wood makes a loud hollow noise as it crashes to the street. The crowd laughs even more, and as they clamor it seems as if they have become one satanic entity, acting in unison. Although there are some who do not join in the ridicule, the majority nearest Jesus do.

The soldiers kick him to get up, but he is so weak and beaten down that they order a man in the crowd to help him to carry the beam. Reluctantly, Simon of Cyrene helps to lift the weight of our burden from his back. Jesus then looks directly into our eyes and speaks.

Beloved, I suffer in this way to give you my strength, Father's strength. Do not let my pain go to waste in your life. As I allow Simon to help me, in your pride do not stop me from helping you. Many times you are worn down and made helpless by trials and testing, even as I am at this moment.

As I allow Simon to share my load, you can see how I share in yours and you share in mine. He, like so many others is reluctant to accept my cross. Learn from me that you need one another from time to time to help you carry your own crossbeam.

I think now of the many who will never take my words or deeds seriously, as there were many who never did. This is a painful aspect of my cross which I have always carried. But just as I already knew that the way of love would not be easy, so too I have made that truth plain to all of my friends. This is not just another way to union with your God — this is the only way, the royal and holy way of the cross. As I humble myself in obedient submission to my Father's will and take up my cross without grumbling, I will raise humanity up to the level of the divine and share that rising with my friends from the past and the present and the future, thus enabling them to reach and touch my Father's glory and beauty.

Father. How I long to be with him, and how my faith and trust in him is sorely put to the test now. Only through him will I be able to continue; I look only to him. Not to this heavy crossbeam, not to my pain-racked body and mind, not even the glory which awaits. My eyes are fixed upon the object of my love, and it is that love which will enable this flesh to rise above the pain, rise above the insults and above the temptations to discouragement. I am keenly aware of my need of him and I am determined to do that which he has given me to do, even unto death.

The soldiers then tell Simon to put the crossbeam back on Jesus' shoulders. Simon seems to have had his own transformation, for there is now compassion in his eyes as he gently puts the beam, our burden, back on Jesus. It is as if his distaste and embarrassment have been turned into tenderness and courage simply by the act of helping Jesus.

The soldiers push Jesus on once again, and within moments his face cringes as his blood-encrusted eyes fill and overflow with tears. About a foot or two away he sees his mother. As she looks at him you can see the intense pain she is experiencing; he can see it also. Between them there is a profound oneness of pain, acceptance and understanding. He is not permitted to stop and she is shoved back and becomes lost in the crowd, left only to follow — her only son, as he labors to give birth to a whole new race of people, just as she labored to give birth to the first-born of all creatures.

As we watch Mary disappear into the mob we hear the ungodly sound of the wood hitting the ground once again. Still he does not cry out or lash out at anyone. There, before our eyes, lies the great Lion of Judah in the dirt of Jerusalem. Our heart aches for love of him — not pity, but love and overwhelming gratitude, as we realize that he does this for us. He reads our hearts and speaks.

Precious friend, just as I can read the love in your heart, so too my Father looks upon my heart in this great distress. I am tempted to doubt his goodness, but even though it is difficult for me now to concentrate, he is so much a part of me I could never forget. I am worn down, but hidden behind my apparent brokenness are a peace and joy which defy logic. He is the source of that. Each step I take under this burden, each fall I endure is a wondrous act of love, no matter how feeble or faltering. He accepts it. He and I are one and his goodness is my own.

I am the Father's goodness, his kindness, his compassion, his love. In the same way, you can be mine.

Please do not lose heart in your own weak struggles, especially when you fail. Through me you can live my humble way of love quite heroically and redemptively. Without me you can do nothing, just as I can do nothing apart from my Father. But if you lean on your own strength, you are doomed to fail.

I call you to choose to live my way — a heroic life of grace — exactly where I have placed you: in the mundane little trials and in the tragic big ones too. Whatever I permit to come into your life, allow me to mold and transform you in them, daily dying to self, self-satisfaction and self-interest. As my Father himself is my stamina, so I promise to be yours.

At this time every person is utterly powerless against the evil of Satan, powerless also to overcome the darkness which lurks within their hearts and minds. Even as all this dark evil presses upon me here, I know that through what I suffer all humanity will be given the freedom to choose to walk the path of life with my own power alive and abiding in them.

The soldiers kick him and pull him up and forward once again, and he staggers towards a group of women who are crying out and beating their breasts. He tries to comfort them even in the midst of his own overwhelming pain, always reaching out, never complaining. The noise and remarks of the crowd cause him great inner pain, for his eyes fill with tears over and over again. Those people, unaware that salvation trips and falls at their very feet, yell obscenities at Jesus as he limps right by them. The endless stream of curses, the undiluted pain from the beating, the extreme mental and physical exhaustion of the walk, the hard falls; it seems incredible that anyone could live through this kind of torture.

He falls again and this time the beam hits the ground and bounces back and hits him on the shoulder as he goes down under its weight. As he lies there, for a moment even the soldiers hesitate to kick him again. He is a mass of blood and wounds. To look at him is frightening, because in him we see the fact of our own sin and brokenness reflected. We are wrapped up and tied to the mystery of this Suffering Servant with cords of divine love, and if we accept his brokenness, then we must accept our own. By his ever-present grace and care he lets us perceive his beauty shining through his unsightly and broken exterior, and all at once we know that Jesus Christ in us is our only hope of glory.

You have learned well, my friend. Golgotha is in my sight. My walk here is almost done; my mission is almost finished. Although this journey to Golgotha is less than half a mile, its benefits are eternal. Just as my steps here have a royal purpose, so do yours. My walk of love here will enable many others just like you, my beloved, to travel the hard and narrow path towards transformation and more perfect union with me. We have arrived in the fullness of time at my place of execution.

Meditation Seven
Golgotha and Beyond

EVEN THOUGH we have now travelled outside the city itself there are still crowds of people following the "procession." As we walk along this most difficult road, we see that although the stony roughness of the street has smoothed out into dirt, it is still very hard for Jesus to endure. His physical stamina is all but gone. It is only the raw power of love which allows him to continue.

The road itself is rising and getting steeper as he feebly stumbles towards his altar of sacrifice. Up on the hill ahead at Golgotha scaffolds loom ominously up out of the earth and stand out starkly against the cloud-studded blue sky.

When we arrive at the spot designated for his execution the guards roughly grab and untie him, remove the sign from around his neck, strip off his clothes and throw him naked to the ground. They move the beam of wood and put it over by the standing frames.

As they get everything ready, Jesus just slumps there in the dirt with his head bowed. Flies are buzzing around his open wounds; his face is swollen, bloody and bruised; very little flesh is left on his entire body which has not been battered or marked in some way. Within, his mind is ravaged, his soul is pierced and his heart is broken. Yet he asks us to come and sit beside him.

My mind is on the point of bursting with pain and sorrow, for there is a great and violent struggle going on within me. Although I am sinless, I experience the full impact of sin within my flesh now as the battle between absolute good and absolute evil takes place within me: the struggle between love and hate, obedience and disobedience, faithfulness and faithlessness, human willfulness and the holy will of God.

As I anticipate further torture, I look around and still I

see and hear the caustic voice of sin as it rages and ravishes my people. I see the tremendous need of my Father's love. The chasm is so great that only he is sufficient to fill it; the gap is so wide only my cross is able to bridge it. The weight of all this steadily increases until it is fully upon me and I am emptied. This is my hour, although it may not appear that way. Even my friends feel that I am defeated and that their hope is gone. If only they would remember my words and cling to them.

They are coming for me. Go now, my beloved, over to my mother. Even as she needs comfort at this moment, so do you. I entrust you to her now. She is my gift to you and you are mine to her, for the rest of what you will see and learn here will be too much for you to bear, except in her arms. Need I say I love you?

Sending us into the arms of blessed Mary, Jesus shows how tenderly he loves us. As the mighty God entrusted his own fragile tiny human frame into the hands of this capable woman, he reserves no less care and treatment for his Church. For it is at this hour that the birth of his Mystical Body takes place, and it is fitting that it is born into the open and obedient arms of his mother — our mother.

Mary is quietly sobbing and intently watching her Son. Even in the midst of this she warmly receives us. As soon as we are safely in her arms they take Jesus and throw him to the ground again, and then they put his hands on top of the large beam of wood: our burden, everyone's burden. With very large spikes they fasten him to it. The sound of the hammer echoes in our ears like thunder over and over again.

After this they take the ropes, which symbolize the binding of us all, and they hoist him up and affix the beam to the frame. Then they hammer nails through his feet too. Painfully, graphically we see that we are indeed carved into his hands and into his feet as well.

In Mary's arms, we see this loving, precious, totally desolate man. As we see our Lord stripped of everything — dignity, honor, respect, friends and home — we realize that he is the very source and foundation of all true humility. In the shadow of the cross we hide in Mary's arms, embarrassed by our own nakedness before our naked God as he hangs stretched out with arms open wide, lashed and pinned to his own creation, eternally beckoning us: Come!

The gentle voice of the One who is saving us all breaks through the noise and confusion which surround us. We can hear his thoughts; not through our ears, but we feel them vibrating deep within our heart.

My Father, forgive them. I will never stop asking you to forgive them. I love them so, Father; you love them too — do not hold this against them. Remember that our love for them is so great because of their weakness, not in spite of it. You know all things, Father. You know that they really do not understand, they do not know what they are doing. They are all as children caught in a maze, a trap. Merciful Father, Abba, you sent me to free them from the snare, to lead them out of the maze into your open arms of tender and compassionate love. This is why you sent me, why I chose to come; this is why I was born. Please, forgive them, forgive them all.

As we hear his heart cry out in this accursed darkness, we realize that his love does not depend on anyone's actions. He lived what he is — the embodiment of love. As his words echo in our ears, his forgiveness floods our hearts. His love is stronger and greater than all of our sins — indeed it is greater and stronger than all the collective sin from the beginning of time to its end.

His thoughts and feelings of love and forgiveness are now shattered by a loud mocking voice from the crowd: "If you are really the Son of God..." The temptations to despair and to use his power selfishly crash over him like ocean waves, relentlessly, one after another. "He trusted in God — "

My God, my God, why have you abandoned me?

His thoughts touch our hearts deeply as he again lets us glimpse the inner sanctum of his brokenness. The pain Jesus experiences in the depth of his apparent abandon-

ment by his Father is the apex of his suffering. In this we see that he has shown us not only the face of love, but the face of sin as well. As the heavy weight of seeming separation from his Father crushes his very soul, we can truly say, "This is sin." We can see how Satan corrupts and perverts God's beauty. We see what sin has done in all its magnitude and what it is capable of, as its tentacles reach into the human mind and heart and separate us from God. Jesus has allowed himself to experience all of sin's rage and has taken nothing or done nothing to dull or ease the pain. The only thing he asks from us in return is that we love him back and live his way of love.

Now as the sky gets darker, it would seem that Satan has won the victory. Yet through my suffering, sin and Satan are irrevocably defeated. My agony is in the thought that not everyone will share in and celebrate my victory.

Beloved, what I anticipated last night at the Passover meal, I fulfill here in order to remain with you always, to give you my power in your struggle with evil, to nourish you on your own walk of love, to be your everlasting Passover. The breaking of this Bread will resound through the ages. For how could I say that I love my friends, that I love you and indeed all people and not act on it? For love without deeds is meaningless, and to lay down one's life is the greatest proof of love that a person can give.

I am man to redeem fallen human nature, to purify humanity from the inside out, to reconcile all people to their God. Yet I am not just any man, so mine is the greatest and most valuable sacrifice of all.

I am the Son of God, his own Lamb who takes away the sin of the world.

I am the reality and the greatest sign of my Father's solemn and eternal Covenant of love with humanity.

Not only by words did I teach my friends about my Father's love: I allowed them to experience his great love in me through the love relationships we formed with one another. Now, by my death I show and prove his love for humanity once and for all!

My beloved friend, can you draw nearer to me and accept my brokenness? Will you share in my suffering and allow me to form and mold you into the pattern of my death so you may share also in my glory? Will you lovingly accept my Father's will in your life as I do, or will you complain and balk at it? These are difficult questions, but you must answer them. I have walked towards Hell itself and towards this hour with fearful anticipation and longing. It has been extremely difficult, but I have faithfully carried your burden in me and with me as I have carried the burden of all people.

Slowly he lifts his head and looks directly at us. Our greatest desire is somehow to put an end to our beloved Friend's horrible suffering. But we are unable to do anything. We are powerless. He knows our thoughts and speaks.

My friend, your helplessness here in this circumstance reveals your great need of me. Although I do suffer tremendously your compassion comforts me greatly, for in you I see the fruit of my labor. Your compassion for me is a reflection of your Father and mine, and it would not be possible if he were not so much a part of you.

I see that my nakedness, too, causes you great distress. Understand that in the same manner in which I was born into this world, I will leave it: humble, naked and hungry.

Part of what you experience as you stand here face to face with your Redeemer is shame, just as Adam felt shame when my Father called out to him after his sin. You see me as the mirror of your own failures, but as I sanctify failure here, I also reflect the hope of your ultimate victory over all your failures and over the ultimate failure, death.

My beloved, this is the reason for which I was born. Do not allow sorrow to overwhelm you, but find it in your heart to rejoice, for my Father has promised that my life will not end here. By my nature it cannot. I am Life, and Life itself can never die.

I make you a promise. Your life will not end in your failures if you follow my way. I entrusted my entire life into the hands of my Father and it is my prayer that this will be the essence of your life as well. My accomplishment here will enable you to do just that. My work here will wash the sorrow of sin from Adam and from all his descendants who will receive it; it will clothe their nakedness with my own glory which will soon burst forth from my tomb into another, much greater garden.

My mission extends far beyond this cross of agony. What you see is my dead body on this cross, but what we share now in conversation flows from my Risen life. My death is not an end, but a beginning:

The beginning of a new life on earth.

A future full of hope for all who will follow my way of love.

A future that will lead to eternal life with our Father in heaven.

Go forth and spread the good news, I am no longer dead, I have overcome your enemy —

I am alive!